My First Science Book

Push and Pull with BIG MACHINES

Nicola Lopetz

A Crabtree Seedlings Book

CRABTREE
Publishing Company
www.crabtreebooks.com

School-to-Home Support for Caregivers and Teachers

This book helps children grow by letting them practice reading. Here are a few guiding questions to help the reader with building his or her comprehension skills. Possible answers appear here in red.

Before Reading:

• What do I think this book is about?
  • *I think this book is about big machines.*
  • *I think this book is about pushing and pulling.*

• What do I want to learn about this topic?
  • *I want to learn about what big machines can do.*
  • *I want to learn about different kinds of big machines.*

During Reading:

• I wonder why...
  • *I wonder why bulldozers can move big rocks.*
  • *I wonder why bulldozers have a blade in front.*

• What have I learned so far?
  • *I have learned that you can push something away to make it move.*
  • *I have learned that if you pull on something you can make it move toward you.*

After Reading:

• What details did I learn about this topic?
  • *I have learned that pushes and pulls are forces that make things move.*
  • *I have learned more force makes an object move farther.*

• Read the book again and look for the vocabulary words.
  • *I see the word **push** on page 6, and the word **pull** on page 12. The other glossary words are found on page 22.*

Table of Contents

Push

Pull

Big Machines Push

We use big **machines** to move things.

We use a bulldozer to move dirt and rocks.

A bulldozer has a big blade to **push** the dirt and rocks to a different place.

blade

Which bulldozer will need to push harder?

SCIENCE WORD

force (FORS):
Something that
pulls or pushes
something else.

Yes, this one. It will have to use more **force** to push the bigger rock.

Big Machines Pull

We use a tractor to
move a wagon.

A trailer is hitched to the tractor so the tractor can **pull** it.

15

Which tractor will need to pull harder?

Yes, this one. It will have to use more force to pull the bigger trailer.

Find Out More About Force

Try using more or less force to make an object move.

1. Use a toy truck or car.
   Give the toy a small push and measure how far it rolls.

2. Start the toy at the same place and give it a big push.

Which push made the toy roll farther?

Now, tie string to the toy truck or car. Try the same experiment with a small and big pull instead. Which force made the toy move farther—a push by a hand or a pull on a string?

What Did You Learn?

Which sentence is not true?

a. Machines are made by people.

b. Machines make work easier.

c. Machines do not help people.

We use a push or a pull to make something move.

True   False

Which rock will need more force to be moved?

a.

b.

c.

Glossary

force (FORS):

A force is something that pulls or pushes something else.

machines (muh-SHEENZ):

Machines are made by people. We use machines to make work easier.

pull (PUL):

To pull is to move something toward you.

push (PUSH):

To push is to move something away from you by pressing against it.

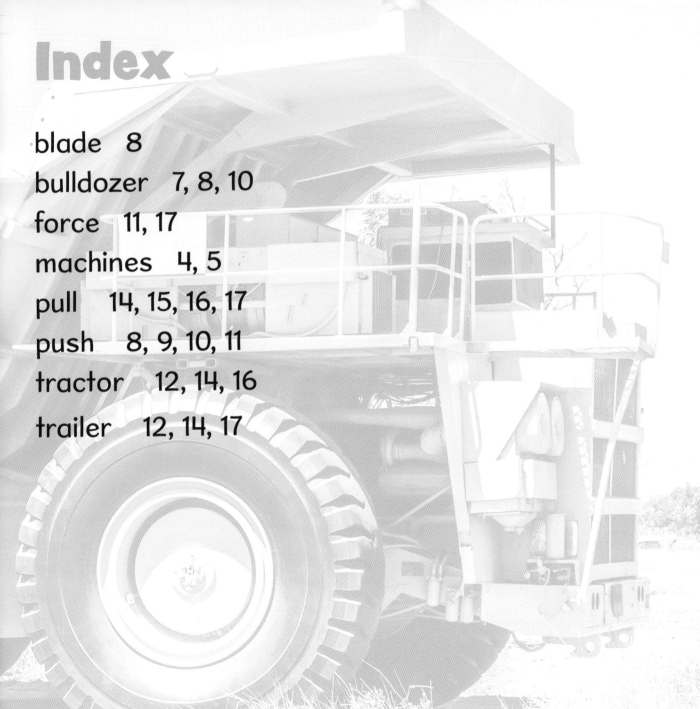

Index

CRABTREE
Publishing Company

Written by: Nicola Lopetz

Print coordinator: Katherine Berti

Photo credits:

Cover ©shutterstock.com/Aleksey, Page 2 ©shutterstock.com/Zdenek Sasek, Page 4/5 ©shutterstock.com/GIRODJL, Page 6/7 ©shutterstock.com/TFoxFoto, Page 8/9 ©shutterstock.com/GIRODJL, Page 10/11 ©shutterstock.com/bulldozer © Vladimir Sazonov, rock © photka, Page 12/13 ©shutterstock.com/jan kranendonk, Page 14/15 ©shutterstock.com/Hansen, Page 16/17 © tractor © shutterstock.com /Photobac, trailer © shutterstock.com / Anatoliy Kosolapav, Page 18/19 ©shutterstock.com/Sabphoto ZouZou, Page 22/23 ©shutterstock.com/M.INTAKUM

Library and Archives Canada Cataloguing in Publication

Title: Push and pull with big machines / Nicola Lopetz.
Names: Lopetz, Nicola, author.
Description: Series statement: My first science books | "A Crabtree seedlings book". | Includes index.
Identifiers: Canadiana (print) 20210203870 |
    Canadiana (ebook) 20210203889 |
    ISBN 9781427159458 (hardcover) |
    ISBN 9781427159533 (softcover) |
    ISBN 9781427160102 (HTML) |
    ISBN 9781427160188 (EPUB) |
    ISBN 9781427160157 (read-along ebook)
Subjects: LCSH: Force and energy—Juvenile literature. |
    LCSH: Earthmoving machinery—Juvenile literature.
Classification: LCC QC73.4 .L66 2022 | DDC j531/.11—dc23

Library of Congress Cataloging-in-Publication Data

Available at the Library of Congress

Crabtree Publishing Company

www.crabtreebooks.com   1-800-387-7650

Print book version produced jointly with Blue Door Education in 2022

Printed in the U.S.A./062021/CG20210401

Published in the United States Crabtree Publishing
347 Fifth Avenue, Suite 1402-145
New York, NY, 10016

Published in Canada Crabtree Publishing
616 Welland Ave.
St. Catharines, Ontario L2M 5V6